KERALA

a magical odyssey

KERALA
a magical odyssey

Photographs by **Sudhir Ramchandran**

Text by **Anita Nair**

TIMELESS BOOKS
New Delhi

This edition published in India in 2005 by

TIMELESS BOOKS
46, Housing Society
South Extension Part-I
New Delhi-110 049 (India)
Tel : 2469 0513, 2469 3257
E-mail : timeless@satyam.net.in

Research head	:	Dr. Sulekha Randhir
Research coordinator	:	Neha Diddee
Caption writer	:	Sonya Thimmaiah
Project Editor	:	Nafisah Ismail
Designer	:	Lynn Chin Nyuk Ling

ISBN : 81-89497-01-4

Printed in Singapore by Fabulous Printers Pte Ltd

To my mother, Mrs. Vimala Ramchandran,

who I adore and whose values I deeply respect,

and my sister Dr Sulekha Randhir, the purity of whose love

I was fortunate to have experienced

Acknowledgements

Several individuals put together this production on Kerala. I thank each one of them for what has emerged in this collection of images that in some way represents my feelings for this wonderful state.

My first and profoundest thanks to my beloved wife, Sandhya, and my gorgeous children, Sapna, Sheetal and Snehal, who stoically tolerated my abrupt and long absences during the photography phase of this project and were my greatest critics.

When in a flux on the flow and structure of the book I could always call on my mother, Vimala Ramchandran, and be assured of receiving sane advice. She had a deep understanding of Keralan culture and traditional values, and I was often the grateful recipient of her sagacity.

My eternal gratitude to my late father Manjerikandy Ramchandran, whose simple truths on life and living guide me to this day. His role was taken over by my late stepfather M.

Chandramouli, who brought us up with understanding and love as though we were his natural-born children.

My fond appreciation to my sister, Dr. Sulekha Randhir, whose work has provided the impetus and core reference material for every image that was shot. She had to pass on during the making of this book. Yet through the difficult final phases of the book I could sense her soothing guidance that made this ten year odyssey a reality. Also to my sister,

Sushma, who was the bulwark that steadied my workplace during my long absences.

I thank all my Keralan relatives for welcoming and taking care of me especially Sithaunty, Uncle Mukundan, Uncle Chandran, Radhaunty, Remachi, Uncle Valsan, Bina, Aunty Vani and Uncle Ram. Also, Uncle Balan, Aunty Shanta, Uncle Bhaskar, Premachi, Leilachi, Raviattan, Joyattan, Kausaunty, Rajuattan and Pushpachi.

An endearing couple I could always count on for insights into the project are Ashok Koshy and his wonderful wife Tilotamma.

My deepest thanks go to my good friend and every photographer's dream, Vasanthi Devagnanam. Despite her frenetic schedule as the director of a leading international corporation, Vasanthi made her editorial and business instincts available to me at various phases of this production. I thank the Devagnanam family, especially Vasanthi's husband, Theo, for facilitating all these interactions with his encouragement.

To my team goes my heartfelt gratitude for their support and friendship through the years it took to create this book. In the beginning there was Parul Shah. An artist par excellence, Parul helped me develop the creative structure of the initial visual content. Subsequently I was assisted by Sanjay Ramachandran and Neha Diddee. They were my inspiration and strength and we formed a dream team. Post photography, Neha kept the editorial continuity flowing with remarkable discipline and innate intuition. Others in my team who provided emotional support and technical photography help were G. Kumaran, Senthil Kumar, Nevil Chitayagam, Srinivas Murthy, Renuka, K. Madhavan, Sunita Philip, Tashina Singh, Soshna Sood and Sudeep Choudhary. I know well how they suffered my idiosyncrasies over this period of time, and I thank them for their patience, in particular M.K. Haridas, who has been an invaluable support for so long and Amanda Tetrault who helped coordinate the intricacies of the prepress stage.

My sincere thanks to Anita Nair, an extremely gifted writer and a well-known novelist of international stature, for having agreed to write the body text for this book.

The captions in the book faithfully communicate both the emotional and historical information of each scene as well as the feelings of the photographer. I thank Sonya Thimmaiah for her indispensable part in telling the story of Kerala as fully as was possible.

The Tourism Director of Kerala during the making of this book, Dr. Venu V. IAS, provided his unstinting support and enthusiasm for the project. Emotions well within me whenever I remember the offer of unlimited free stay for me and my team at the Casino Group of Hotels by George and Jose, the wonderful Dominic brothers, and Mr. Suresh Iyer, vice-president of Kodak, who gifted me with film material that eased some of the fiscal burden of this venture.

I am also indebted to Bipin Shah of Mapin Publications and Edward Booth Clibborn of Clibborn Publications, who counselled me often. As did my close friends Brian and Margaret, Shova Loh, Paul Rozario and Leela Vengaldasam.

The gene of a high quality print production is always a great scan. The A.SANI KW Pre-Press Specialists led by Tony Ooi Kok Pin and his highly skilled professional team of Albert Ooi Chin Choon, Loo Yeok Yeng and Lim Eng Geok rendered plates of high technical excellence and immense tonal values.

The ultimate showcase is the print. Interpreting the mood of a picture and orchestrating the color channels of a high end Heildelberg transcends the craft of printmaking into the realm of fine art. Boon Eow's superlative print effort has breathed life into this body of work.

Lynn Chin of Times Editions has designed a platform for my story that is remarkebly simple in its concept and yet extremely effective. I couldn't have asked for more.

I owe my deep appreciation to K.R. Bilimoria, my friend for over three decades, for pictorial guidance and creative insights; Honnappa Jayadeva, my sagacious sounding board and good friend; and D. Radhakrishnan, my most consistent friend and guide with whom I indulged in photographic banters over the years. My thanks to Tarun Jung Rawat for creating the first complete book design that got me noticed by my publisher.

The seed of the book was sown when my late uncle M. Gopalan, a well-known industrialist from Dar es Salaam, Tanzania, talked to me when I was a child about this beautiful state and the potential of its people. I deeply respect his wife, Aunty Shakuntala, and have fond memories of a childhood spent with his children, mostly with Venu and Neena.

Over several interactions I developed a deep respect for David Yip, my publisher. He was always encouraging and obliging to the wildly fluctuating demands of an unpredictable artist like myself. Nafisah Ismail, my editor, was always a pleasure to talk to, and is owed my thanks for her diligence and the eagle-eyed care she devoted to the progress of the book.

Everyone I met along the way to creating Kerala: A Magical Odyssey is responsible in some way or other for my vision of Kerala. Most of all I thank Kerala and her people for providing the ceaseless inspiration.

Introduction

I am one of those Indians who was born and brought up outside the country in an environment that was alien to Indian culture. My parents are from Kerala, a tiny state in southwestern India. My only initiation into Malayalam, the Keralan language, was a few words that I learnt at a local club in Dar es Salaam when I was very little. Through stories my mother told us we learnt of the characters in the Ramayana, the sacred Indian epic, and of how the Hindu religious book, the Bhagavad-Gita, came about.

I sailed into India at the age of 16 in the bottom deck of an ocean liner, fearful of a country that I did not know, and was completely overawed by the vast Indian Ocean at night. We docked at the beautiful, sparsely populated island of Seychelles, and I remember thinking to myself that if this is what I was going to see halfway to India, the Indian experience couldn't be so frightful after all. Docking in Bombay was a shocking experience as I disembarked into a wall of babbling humanity. I simply did not know what had hit me. A week later I landed in Kerala, a beautiful green and quiet state, where life lazily passed by people, animals and nature.

I spent two years in Kozhikode in the north of Kerala and another three years in Trivandrum, the capital of Kerala, in the south. During this period I graduated in the Sciences and in my understanding of the state and its people. Kerala is a literate state, and I was often amazed at the knowledge of past and current events that even an octogenarian priestess or little children of the fisherfolk possessed. I joined groups that discussed politics fiercely and had an opinion on almost everything. I realised that often in Kerala a person is measured based on his level of knowledge, wit and sarcasm.

Equality between men and women is intrinsic in the character of every Keralan. The Mannarasala Temple in the south of Kerala is one of the only temples in India that is headed by a priestess. Kerala has a matriarchal system, and often in a household of joint families it is the women who make most of the crucial decisions and guide children along their career paths. However, parents strictly forbid young boys and girls talking to each other, and this prudery

has resulted in overt sexuality in Malayalam literature and films.

Every Keralan household strives to be self-sufficient. Affluence is measured by the number of coconut trees in one's compound. Apartments that have begun to sprout recently were a rarity even five years ago. Everyone had individual homes with sufficient land to grow coconuts. The ubiquitous coconut has been put to ingenious use in Kerala and is used in food and home furnishings. It is understood that a girl from a household with more coconut trees could be reasonably certain of securing a well-to-do husband.

My love for the verdant nature of the state grew incrementally as I stayed on. When I returned to Kerala after a stint outside the country, I decided to photograph the state, to capture on film one of the few remaining areas in India where the bounty of nature lay unblemished. I love the clean air that signalled the crossing over of

the borders into Kerala. Often my assistants, Neha and Sanjay, and I would lie on our backs in the deep forests of the Western Ghats, refreshing ourselves and cleansing momentarily the pollutants we had gathered from our urban existence.

The entire state, including the cities, has a rural feel about it. The beauty of the gushing Athirapally Falls during the monsoon is to be felt rather than seen. I can still hear the sound of its falling waters across the round grey rocks at its base, still see the golden sun's rays streaking across the greens of the river bank backlighting the leaves with a rich translucence and still feel the soft wind caressing us while the splendid azure sky fought to retain its colours against the vivid setting sun. The scene is so alive in me and is one of many memorable experiences of my ten-year photographic sojourn in Kerala. Sometimes the camera was an obstruction to the feelings that I had, and the glory of a fabulous sunset or the majesty of a towering elephant was sacrificed to my obsession with capturing the scene on film.

I have always lost myself in the spice jungles and tea estates of Munnar. On every occasion I have felt how true the ancient legend of Lord Parasurama creating Kerala with a throw of his axe into the sea and the rising of this virgin land is. Thekkady is as Eden must have been. Elephants swimming in groups, large numbers of herbivores, such as socked bison and wild boar, moving in mixed herds, and flocks of migratory birds from Eurasia and other distant places dot the Periyar basin. We sighted the shy Nilgiri tahr, and the iridescent feathers of peacocks often brushed our vehicles as we passed by. Trees of every description and rare plants, including a huge reservoir of orchid species, exist here.

I was hardly seven when I saw my first stage drama. There was a fearsome, multicoloured, horrific-looking individual prancing around the stage with a female counterpart, enacted by a man. Over the years, as I watched these complex performances across the globe, my understanding of the Kathakali art form deepened. Today I watch with pride the unfolding of the *Ramayana* epic as colours clash along with cymbals, gestures stab the air and feet stamp the footboards to staccato chanting in the wild frenzy of a Kathakali dance drama.

With my African background I could never envisage a man atop an elephant. It is amazing how the gentle counterparts to the fierce African pachyderms have become almost a part of everyday Keralan life. Elephants and their attendant mahouts are everywhere, from the ritualistic ceremonies of a temple festival to the less honourable task of moving logs in wood depots. Elephants are even used to capture and train other elephants.

Most Indian elephants are trained by Keralan mahouts and come from the deep jungles of the Western and Southern Ghats. In Kerala, the mere sight of this large creature is believed to portend good fortune.

To truly experience Kerala, I think one has to do what I did: travel the *edavazhi*, or narrow pathways, on a motorbike, smell the tea in the early morning at the Munnar mountainside, savour the tapioca and fish curry at a wayside shack, feel the cold, sparkling flow of the backwaters, breathe in the pristine air of a sleepy fishing village and interact with her warm and opinionated people. No wonder National Geographic Traveler Magazine declared Kerala one of the world's 10 natural paradises.

For me, Kerala will always be my own paradise on earth. Through my pictures I hope to share some of her beauty and intricacies of character with the world.

Contents

Paradise *18–31*   Land *32–47*   Water *48–77*

Traditions *78–109*　　　Gods *110–133*　　　Living *134–153*

Paradise

At 1,600 metres above sea level, the idyllic slopes of Munnar in Idukki were a favourite colonial summer escape in pre-independence India. Its profusion of tea gardens are among the highest in the world and imparts to the hill station its vivid greens. Once every 12 years these wonted greens are rivalled by the flowering of the Neelakurinji, a rare plant that bestows upon these mountains an uncommon blue cast.

It is said that thousands of years ago the world was tyrannised by the Kshatriyas, and everyday thousands of innocent men, women and children were killed, maimed or punished for no fault. Kartavirya, their king, had obtained the boon of invincibility, a thousand arms and a golden chariot that went wherever he willed it to go. He would meet his death only at the hands of a man known to the whole world. In grief, the people turned to

Lord Vishnu and pleaded for help. And so Vishnu was born to a sage called Jamadagni. Even as a young lad, Vishnu performed such severe austerities that Lord Shiva, the god of death and destruction, appeared before him and taught him the use of arms. As his personal weapon, Shiva gave him an axe that once raised, would rest only when it had destroyed his opponent. And thus Vishnu came to be known as Parasurama, or Rama with the Axe.

One day Parasurama, his brothers and their father were away from the hermitage they lived in when Kartavirya visited. The villagers welcomed the king and entertained him well. But the king repaid their hospitality by taking away the sacrificial calf. Parasurama returned to find his mother in tears. So he went looking for Kartavirya. "Your tenure has come to an end," Parasurama hollered. "Never again will you oppress harmless folk. Never again will you rule the world with fear."

With his axe, Parasurama cut off all the thousand arms of Kartavirya and then killed him.

Parasurama, whose anger had the power to reduce the world to ashes, then retired to a forest to meditate and calm his mind. While he was in the forest, however, Kartavirya's sons came to the hermitage and killed Jamadagni to avenge their father's death.

Now Parasurama's anger could no longer be checked and he took an oath to cleanse the world of the demonic Kshatriyas. He went around the world 21 times to kill all the Kshatriyas and filled five large lakes with their blood.

Content that his work had been done, Parasurama went to the western coast of the land and flung his axe into the ocean.1 From the waters emerged a thin strip of land where rivers flowed, elephants and deer roamed, birds sang, rare flowers bloomed, and pepper, cardamom and sandalwood scented the air. This was a land where all was green, lush and serene. A resting place born out of restlessness. God's own country raised by the hands of a man. Kerala.

If this is the mythical genesis of Kerala, geology claims that there were at least two stages of land rise from the sea. Seismological movements or volcanic actions created the first mass of land, and rivers depositing large quantities of silt and mud from the mountains created the second land mass. At the same time ocean currents caused sand to pile on the shore.2

In this narrow ribbon of land flanked by mountains on one side and the Arabian Sea on the other are customs, traditions, manners and practices that have no bearing with the rest of the country. Almost as if it has remained insular to all that was happening elsewhere and as if it had risen from the sea as a fully-formed independent being. It is this that makes the ancient Parasurama legend almost believable.

It is said that Parasurama, having raised the land from the sea, decided to populate it with 64 Brahmin families. But the Brahmins disputed

Lotuses flourish in Pookot Lake, a freshwater lake in Wayanad. The lake is surrounded by lush hills on three sides and is a popular picnic spot made more attractive by the absence of human habitation or industry.

Elephants mimic synchronised swimmers with surprising grace at the Periyar Wildlife Sanctuary. Lake tours allow thrilling proximity to the animals and laudable government efforts have replaced the small, polluting diesel boats with battery-operated, non-intrusive tourist vessels. The sanctuary is home to approximately 800 elephants, which make for fascinating herd dynamics.

Left: Paddy fields ribbon across Kerala's landscape and are significant contributors to the lush appeal of the state.

Preceding page: The graceful and magnificent Athirapally Falls near Thrissur, like a mystical lady dressed in white, plunge from a height of 80 feet to the delight of visitors from all over the country. The existence of these breathtaking falls is being threatened by a power generation project.

among themselves, and in sheer desperation to prevent anarchy and chaos they decided to invite rulers from across the mountains. The Brahmins decided that these rulers would each preside only for 12 years to avoid monarchies or dictatorships. Ironically enough these rulers were Kshatriyas and came to be known as Perumals. The first Perumal was called a Keralan.[3]

But just as one begins to shake one's head in disbelief and starts dismissing the story as a mere legend, history rears its head. The first reference to Kerala is in an edict engraved on a rock by Emperor Asoka between 272 B.C. and 232 B.C.[3] Kerala owes its origins to the word Keralaputra, which means Land of the Sons of Cheras. The Cheras were the first large empire to take roots in this state.[4]

A dawn still life in the placid backwaters of Malabar in northern Kerala. Fishing boats, palms and backwaters are perhaps the words that are most evocative of the striking landscapes of rural Kerala.

However, artefacts dating back to 4000 B.C. point to the existence of a highly developed ancient culture in Kerala.[3] There are burial stones and urns, microliths, stone records and copper plates. Ancient Keralans used stone or copper to record data till the end of the 14th century. Palm leaves took over as the medium of records until the 19th century, though paper was already in use as early as in the 16th century.[3]

The origin of this state and its name might hover in that uncertain terrain between myth and reality, but what is undisputed is the sheer natural magnificence of Kerala. From the majestic heights of the Western Ghats, the land undulates westward towards the Arabian Sea and creates a landscape of valleys draped in varied shades of green. Many rivers weave their way through these hills to merge their waters with the sea. Along the coast there are lagoons and backwaters sheltered by sand dunes. The quiet of this enchanted world is broken only by the coos of koels, the rasping cries of Indian tree magpies and the fluttering wings of cranes. It is as if nature knew no limits when it decided to bequeath its bounty to this land. And it is one of nature's gifts that charted the course of Kerala's vivid but checkered history.

We need to step back in time to understand this. There is the legend of how the Queen of Sheba, when she decided to go to Jerusalem and present herself, carried in her train "spices, gold, precious stones and the wood of the almug tree", or sandalwood, from Ophir. Historians claim that Ophir

Untouched by human hands, the pristine Kunthipuzha River gurgles through Silent Valley National Park. It is the only river in South India with a course exceeding 20 km that does not pass through a single human settlement.

could be the ancient, submerged town of Puhar in Kerala.[5]

It is to the same period of history that the temples and palaces of the Babylonian king Nebuchadnezzar belong. Remnants of the buildings that have surfaced as a result of archaeological digs show these to be hardwoods that perhaps came from the tropical forests of Kerala.

The first reference to pepper appears in Roman history and can be dated to the first century when Pliny the Elder remarked that "the Roman nobility were depleting the treasury with their greed for pepper."[5] It is this greed for pepper that brought ships into the ports of Malabar. More interestingly

it is this trade in pepper and other spices that provide the first hints of the political history of the region that later became known by such names as Venad, Kochi, Malabar, Travancore-Cochin and finally as Kerala state.

While trade between India and the Western world had existed for many centuries, what made Malabar so tradeworthy, apart from it being a cornucopia of spices, was the discovery of the monsoon winds by Greek sailors in A.D. 45. The sailors discovered that by harnessing the monsoon winds from the Horn of Plenty in Africa, it was possible to sail to Malabar in just 45 days. Soon Muziris, which stood at the mouth of the Periyar river and whose location was where Kodungalloor stands today, became a busy port and facilitated trade with the Greeks, Arabs, Europeans and Chinese.

Vasco da Gama's landing at Kappad on the Malabar Coast in 1498 started a rash of colonialisation by the

Dutch, Portuguese, French and British. Meanwhile the peppercorn once more triggered off events in Europe that changed the course of Kerala's history and to some extent India's. The British East India Company came into being in 1599 when the Dutch hiked the price of pepper by one shilling.

The British East India Company annexed Kerala as a British colony by signing a strategic treaty with King Marthanda Varma in 1723. British rule lasted almost two centuries and ended in 1947.[5]

Kerala in its present form came into existence only in 1956 when new states were formed based on the geographical distribution of languages in India. The regions of Travancore, Kochi and Malabar were combined into one to be called Kerala.

Who would imagine that a tiny peppercorn could determine the shaping of a land's past triumphs and failures?

The peppercorn still thrives. So does cardamom, rubber, coconut, coffee, tea, paddy and tapioca. An abundance that lures the world now as it did then.

In fact if one of the ancient travellers were to return to Kerala, he would discover that while much has changed, the essence of Kerala continues to be the same. That of a race that is a conundrum by itself. A race that is defined by the language it speaks: Malayalam. And so a person from Kerala is called a Malayali.

On the one hand the Malayali finds contentment in little things: his daily splash in a river or pond, laundered white clothes, a bowl of rice and fish curry and the ownership of his own patch of land with its grove of coconut trees.

Yet this is also a voluble vocal race that lets no industry thrive, for everyone knows their rights and demands that they be met. Communism lives alongside capitalism. Marx is read by the same man who swears by the Bible or the Bhagavad-Gita. Animist practices coexist with organised religion. Ancient art forms such as Kalaripayattu and Kathakali enjoy pride of place with experimental theatre and parody shows.

Jaded and weary a traveller arrives at Kerala and finds a haven. In its valleys and backwaters, dreams are spun as coir is.

In the span of a few days the traveller is introduced to a world that is unique and perhaps unreal. The acquaintance that follows is based on a smattering of carefully packaged experiences. "This is Kerala," they think. This abundance, this many-hued green, this land with its rich folklore and caparisoned elephants.

But the real Kerala remains undiscovered. Untouched and unvoiced, it waits for you to seek it and find it....

Above: A white sari, a thick braid of hair interlocked with a string of jasmine flowers, a chain around the neck and a welcoming charm characterise the typical Keralan girl. Kerala has the highest literacy levels in all of India for both men and women. Many women have capitalised on this privilege by launching careers for themselves in industries such as information technology and hospitality.

Right: People from the backwaters of Palazhi village in Kozhikode reveal their contemplative sides in the shade of coconut palms. The agrarian life is typically exhausting with dawn-to-dusk days spent labouring in the fields.

ഭൂമി

LAND

Sahadevan, a rubber tapper at the Kalarickal estate in Kottayam, makes an expert half-spiral incision into the bark of a rubber tree. The milky sap that oozes from the incision, commonly called latex, is collected in a receptacle tied to the trunk of the tree. Kottayam is commonly known as the Land of Letters, Lakes and Latex owing to its numerous educational institutions and 100 percent literacy rate; the presence of Vembanad Lake, the largest lake in Kerala; and its production of 95 percent of India's rubber yield.

Perhaps understanding Kerala ought to begin with understanding the lay of its land. Hemmed in by the Western Ghats on its eastern side and flanked by the Arabian Sea on the other side, Kerala runs 580 kilometres along the western coast, is 121 km at its widest and a mere 32 km at its narrowest. The tall mountains made Kerala almost inaccessible by land until the 15-km-wide Palakkad gap in the Western Ghats was discovered.

Geographically Kerala can be divided into three regions: mountains, laterite hills and coastal plains. The highlands are home to tea, coffee, rubber and cardamom plantations. In the hills and valleys, crops such as cashew, coconut and pepper are intensively cultivated. The coastal area consists of river deltas and backwaters, where the people depend on fishing and the cultivation of coconuts and rice for their livelihood.[6]

There are 24 million people living on 38,863 square kilometres of Keralan land. One-sixth of this land is forested and is where mahogany, sandalwood, teak and rosewood still grow.[7] Before the birth of Christianity teak wood from Kerala was used for the construction of buildings in places such as Ur in Mesopotamia (present-day Iraq) and later in the construction of British ships used by Admiral Horatio Nelson in the battle of Trafalgar against Napoleon Bonaparte in 1805.

Of the rest of the land, most of it is cultivated and with maximum efficiency. Away from the plains and laterite hills where rice, coconut and rubber reign is the planting country. It is a land where jungle trails and footpaths through cultivated areas still outnumber roads. It is a land of few roads, and almost each one of them is a winding, twisting climb to nowhere. It is a land of breathtaking splendour.

There is a strange clear beauty of form about the mountains. They are large, imposing and grimly handsome. They stand set back and shrouded in a clear, frosty air as if each one of them would isolate itself further and forever from the landscape. Giant shadows hold the damp blue mountains in their grip. The mountainous land that is Kerala's plantation country was once inaccessible tracts of tall grass, thick jungles and malaria-infested marshes. The early planters cleared them to create the first plantations.

Elephants, it has been recorded, are the finest roadmakers in the world,

Groups of women sow paddy in Kuttanad, Alappuzha. Kuttanad is often referred to as the rice bowl of Kerala. In rural India, arduous field labour is often the responsibility of the female members of the family. Rice is the staple food of the state, and swathes of sun-burnished paddy emblazon the landscape of Kerala.

Above: In a ginger warehouse in Jew Town, Fort Kochi, mounds of ginger are gunnysacked and auctioned off as they have been for hundreds of years. Little has changed in this part of Jew Town where beguiling aromas negate the need for warehouse addresses. With Kochi a major port, spices from all over Kerala linger briefly in the warehouses before being snapped up by the lucrative export market.

Left: Women pick cardamom on one of many plantations in Kerala. Cardamom is exported

to various parts of the world for sparing use in cuisine, perfumery, medicines and beverages. Vandanmedu town in Thekkady holds one of the largest cardamom auctions in the world.

Above: The weathered foreman of the ginger warehouse takes a brief respite on a hectic day.

and the early planters followed the trails made by the elephants. They built grass huts to live in, shot a variety of small game to live on, brought in labour from the plains and tried to keep them from running away from the bone-chilling damp and the almost palpable fear all around when even the moon had a devilish cast to it. There was a sense of momentariness and expectation. As though some dramatic occurrence was about to take place. An upheaval, an explosion, a furrowing of the horizon...all they knew was that they were glad to be part of it. It is from such efforts that many of today's giant estates came into being.

Misty, lush-green and nearly 1,600 metres above sea level in the Annamalai range of Kerala is Munnar, a tea plantation centre. It stands at the confluence of three rivers. *Moonu* and *aar* mean three and river in Tamil respectively. Hence the name Munnar.

Tea gardens, some of the highest in the world, stretch up the sides of the hills and are interspersed with pockets of forest rich in wildlife. Munnar from above spreads like a vast bonsai garden stretching to the end of the horizon and provides a vivid contrast to coastal, palm-fringed Kerala. Since the 30-odd tea gardens around Munnar are all privately owned, the colonial town itself is beautifully maintained and has its own charm.

While the tropical forests are inhabited by elephants, tigers, deer and gaurs, the hills surrounding Munnar are home to one of the world's rarest mountain goats, the Nilgiri tahr.

Rather like the koel's call, one of the constants of life in Kerala is the sound

in size, the state produced 25 percent of India's coffee in 1997 and 1998.

Top: The smell of fragrant coffee blossoms in Wayanad fill the air after the mid-year showers. Coffee is the second largest traded commodity in the world after oil. Although most coffee plantations in Kerala are less than two hectares

Right: The clouds subside with the rise of the sun and a spectacular morning unfurls over a Munnar tea plantation. Although tea plants grow to heights of up to 30 feet, regular pruning maintains them at between 4 and 5 feet, which is the ideal height for tea pickers. Trees are often planted between the tea plants for microclimatic benefits and soil improvement.

of the cicadas. And yet there is a place where the cicadas do not sing: Silent Valley, so named by the British for the absence of the cicadas.

The local name for the park is Sairandhrivanam, or the Forest in the Valley. This and the fact that the Kunthipuzha River drains into it give the valley a mythological dimension.

Silent Valley is located in the Kundali Hills of the Western Ghats and is a national park that has an astonishing array of rare plants and herbs. More importantly, this is the last virgin tract of tropical evergreen forest in India. Though smaller in size compared to the other national parks in India, what makes it unique is its green belt.

This green belt almost never came to be because the Kerala State Electricity Board wanted to build a project in the area in the 1970s. As this project would have caused much damage to the ecosystem of the national park, political lobbies and environmentalists rallied together and the plan was set aside. In 1984 Silent Valley, which includes the project area, was proclaimed a national park. Finally in 1986 the park became the core area in the Nilgiri Biosphere Reserve.[8]

Though the cicadas do not sing here, Silent Valley is full of other species of wildlife and their sounds. From peninsular mammals to over a hundred species of butterflies, Silent Valley is home to many yet-to-be-classified species of flora and fauna.[9]

It is almost impossible to think of Kerala without thinking of elephants. In fact, there is a saying that when the last descendant of the Travancore family dies, so will the elephant in Kerala. Such is its link with the land, the people and traditions that an elephant has many a role to play in the everyday life of Kerala. There is the temple elephant whose domain is the temple and streets. There is also the working elephant used in logging camps and by the forest department as employees entitled to salaries in the form of feeds and pensions after a certain age.

Nevertheless elephants in the wild

Right: A bull elephant contemplates the jungle in solitude. Bull elephants break from their herds upon attaining sexual maturity to travel either on their own or in groups of bachelors called bull bands. Elephant herds are matriarchal with the oldest and most experienced female assuming the role of leader. Among Asian elephants, only the males grow tusks, unlike African elephants whose tusks are gender-independent.

Preceding page: A hammer slung over his shoulder in place of his usual school bag, a young boy heads off into the tea plantations in Munnar. Life in the mountains often involves youngsters working on the plantations with their families and simultaneously pursuing educations that will provide them with a greater variety of career options in the future.

Left: The Nilgiri tahr is an endangered species of mountain goat found in South India. Rampant poaching had reduced the numbers of this shy animal to below a hundred at the start of the 20th century. Concerted conservation efforts brought their numbers in India up to around 2,500 in the year 2000. The Eravikulam National Park in Idukki was established in 1978 as a sanctuary for the Nilgiri tahr.

Above: The Periyar Wildlife Sanctuary in Thekkady, Idukki, extends across 777 km² and nurtures over 1,965 flowering species. Wildlife enthusiasts from all parts of the world, who are drawn to Periyar on the promise of herds of wild elephants cavorting in Periyar Lake, rarely leave disappointed. Sambar, flying squirrels and gaurs, or Indian bison, are commonly spotted at the sanctuary.

continue to be threatened by poachers. To preserve the wild elephant and other species of wildlife, the government has established numerous wildlife sanctuaries all over Kerala. The Eravikulam National Park was established specially for the preservation of the Nilgiri tahr, one of the most endangered animals on the planet. Now the number of tahrs in Eravikulam National Park has increased and makes up the largest-known population of tahrs existing in the world.

The entire district of Wayanad is a wildlife sanctuary and its hills throng with elephant stories. Here one can encounter Andy Warhol's theory of 15 minutes of fame. In Wayanad the road to celebrityville begins with the elephant. Almost everyone has an elephant tale to tell, elephant wisdom to disseminate, elephant theories to propound and at least one I-don't-know-how-I-lived-to-tell-you-this encounter with an elephant.

Sultan Bathery, the last outpost of the district, is just another small town in Kerala. Its uniqueness does not extend beyond the *kinnath appam*, which is a steamed pudding made of rice flour, jaggery and coconut milk.

However, Sultan Bathery has plenty of everything else: plastic buckets, duck eggs, jewellery, cast iron skillets and purple seedless grapes from Sangli. Add to this the knowledge that the shops are just a façade. Behind it is the jungle, a dark slumbering beast. During the day monkeys dart through its leafy limbs. At night, it comes alive with a certain stealthiness. A jackal yowls.... [1]

Despite the government's efforts, some species of wildlife have become extinct and many others are endangered. The animals' only serious enemy is man and his need to encroach into their territory. And yet, it isn't as if the average Malayali is a landlocked being. If land is the terra firma of life, it is water that determines the course of progress.

Tribal men in the Periyar settlement work in the forests and agricultural fields as daily wage earners, while the women are responsible for domestic duties such as the pounding of grain, their staple food.

WATER

Distinctive Chinese nets line the waterfront at Kochi in Ernakulam. The nets lining the harbour are called *cheena vallam* and have been in use for over 600 years, but now they yield a meagre catch because of overfishing. The graceful dropping in and lifting out of the nets from the water when they are in operation suggests a paying of respects to the sea for each catch.

Imagine a land, its people, its economy and its everyday harnessed to the rise and fall of tides…this then is Kerala. A place made up of 40 percent water and 60 percent land. Crisscrossed by many rivers and over a thousand canals. Most are almost entirely monsoon-fed, which means the rivers and canals fluctuate in size and power from season to season.

The monsoon, perhaps even more than politics, has a way of taking over daily life in Kerala. Such is its omnipresence that it hijacks even conversation. So that all that is discussed is its time and manner of arrival—with a big bang that drenches anything and everything in its path, its intensity or sometimes the lack of it.

The monsoon first arrived in India

Above: A German couple enjoys a deserted expanse of private beach at Somatheeram Ayurvedic Beach Resort in Thiruvananthapuram. The award-winning resort is a magnet for European tourists seeking a restorative holiday.

Above: The sky and sea hurl temper tantrums at each other in the period that marks the arrival of the monsoon. Even the Kovalam Beach lighthouse, perched at its elevated level, seems vulnerable to the twin furies.

Above and right: A monsoon begins at Varkala Beach. A brow of menacing clouds in an amber sky gives way to a downpour and veritable merging of sky and sea. Kerala is the first state in India to receive the southwesterly monsoon.

during the Miocene epoch between five million and 24 million years ago. The cause seems to have been the mighty uplift of the Himalayas and the Tibetan plateau. Owing to its proximity to the Arabian Sea, Kerala is the first state each season to receive the monsoon rains, which contribute significantly to its 118 inches of annual rainfall. The onset of monsoon in Kerala is eagerly awaited by the rest of India, which is baking under the heat of summer.

What scientific data will not reveal and is part of local folklore is the capricious nature of the southwest monsoon. Of how it almost always breaks on the day schools reopen after the summer vacations. So that children, in their new uniforms, carrying new bags and holding aloft new umbrellas, have to negotiate the puddles on the roads. Of rain that waits for clothes to be hung out on lines to dry, or for people to leave their homes without umbrellas before it comes

hurtling down, persisting vigorously till everything is wet and sodden before it stops with the same abruptness with which it began.

Every year the monsoon breaks at Kovalam, the much-celebrated beach 12 km away from Thiruvananthapuram. From there the monsoon begins its journey northwards. To Varkala Beach, Kollam, Alleppey, Kochi and moving up the coast rapidly, leaving a trail of wetness behind.

While much of Kerala's life

Above: Kovalam is one of Kerala's most popular beaches and draws the crowds during peak seasons. The first outsiders to discover the beach in the 1970s were hippies, but today it attracts more mainstream visitors. The restaurants that line the bay are packed owing to their dual lure of fresh seafood and live traditional dance performances.

Left: The placidity of the beach in the morning is not indicative of the throb of daily life at work. Mornings are the busiest part of a fisherman's day, when the catch is secured.

Preceding page: Coconut kernel is dried to copra for use in Keralan cuisine. The abundance of coconuts in Kerala has engendered uses for each and every part of the coconut—from the use of its leaves in thatching and handicrafts to the fermentation of its sap to brew toddy.

Below: Fishermen begin their day early and are seen hauling in their catches at dawn.

revolves around its freshwater trails, its coast is no less important. In fact, Kerala has some of India's finest beaches. Take Kovalam, a small fishing village named for its grove of coconut trees. Today it has sun worshippers from all over the world seeking its spread of surf and sand. Kovalam's most popular beach is Lighthouse Beach. It is from the middle beach called Hawah that local fishermen set sail every morning. Samudra, the quietest of these, is speckled with a few boats and fewer people. However, Kovalam also has its ugly sides. Erosion has eaten away at the beach, and the ugliness of drugs and sex trafficking, at its ambience.[10]

Left: A setting sun leaves behind its trail of gold over the port of Beypore. Beypore is a famed shipbuilding centre with a 1,500-year-old tradition and is renowned for the construction of the *uru*, an Arabian trading vessel.

Below: A trio of friends revels in a moonlit night on Varkala Beach.

Kovalam is not the only beach to cast a spell. While there are many beaches, the most important ones owe their prominence to historic and religious reasons. There is Varkala Beach, which is considered to be holy. It is also known as Papanashini, meaning that which destroys sins.[11] Then there is Alleppey Beach, a spectacular stretch of sand rimmed with dense coconut groves.

The beach of historical importance is Kappad, where Portuguese navigator Vasco da Gama landed in 1498 and subsequently changed the course of Indian history. About 16 km away from Kozhikode, the pleasant and calm beach, locally known as Kappakadavu, is dotted with rocks and caressed by gentle waves.[11]

Further north is Bekal Beach, where Bekal Fort, one of the largest forts in Kerala, is located.

While the beaches alone were enchanting enough to lure travellers, what brought forth visitors increasingly was trade. Kerala's seafront was studded with port cities

Women sort shrimps brought ashore by the men according to size. A book by the name *Chemmeen*, or *The Shrimps*, written by Thakazhi Sivasankara Pillai, is one of the masterpieces of Keralan literature. The book was adapted into an award-winning film of the same title. The story tells a tragic tale of the lives of fishing folk intertwined with the wrath of the sea.

that even to this day continue to be trade zones.

Kollam was a port used by travellers such as Ibn Batuta and by the Phoenicians, Romans and Chinese. The Portuguese, Dutch and British also set up trading centres here.[12]

When the sea retreated from Kottayam and Tripunitura and the ancient port of Muziris became silted up in 1341, a great deal of the trade shifted to Kochi.

Facing the backwaters is Ernakulam, the district headquarters and an important commercial and residential area. Kochi Shipyard, the biggest shipbuilding yard in India, is situated in the southern part of Ernakulam near Willingdon Island.

Further north is Kozhikode, a city that has always conjured images of exotica. Calico, a fine variety of handwoven cotton cloth said to have originated from this place, is derived from the old city's name, Calicut.[13]

Apart from being trading centres, the coastline of Kerala has spawned other occupations. While fishing and the production of coconut oil and pressed oil cakes from coconut seeds were a thriving industry, the most significant one was boatbuilding.

There is a curious sound that reverberates through the alleys of Beypore, which is 8 km from Kozhikode. A rhythm that is hard to place. A resonance that is both familiar and strange. You think you know it. And then you think you don't. In the end when you see the source of that

pagan beat for yourself, you wonder why it never occurred to you that this music that had teased and taunted you was the note of wood on wood.

Alongside the Chaliyam river estuary that flows into the Arabian Sea lies the secret history of Beypore: its ancient boatyard.

According to Captain Iwata, founder member of the Association of Sumerian ships in Japan, Beypore had direct links with Mesopotamia and was probably a major stop in the maritime Silk Route. In fact he believes that Sumerian ships might have been built in Beypore. So when Captain Iwata set

out to prove that a maritime trade link did exist between Mesopotamia and other countries, it is to Beypore he came to build his dream ship some years ago. The ship in which he would trace the famed Silk Route.

Built according to a design recorded on a Sumerian cuneiform tablet preserved at the Louvre museum, the 3,000-tonner is made entirely of wood. Its planks are held together by wooden nails and coir yarn. A special glue made of fruit and tree resins is used for additional bonding, and the anchor is hewn out of granite. While there was some

Above left: A lone ferry represents the only sign of marine activity in an otherwise bustling Kochi seafront. Red-tiled roofs, undulating palms and frenetic waterfront activities typify the cityscape of Kochi. Many theories abound on the name, the most literal being that it is a derivative of *kaci*, which means harbour in Tamil.

Above right: A dipping sun heightens the romance of a serene pool paralleling the swirling sea. The Brunton Boatyard in Fort Kochi is an intimate resort hotel that was once a fully functional boatyard.

Left: An *uru* awaits the finishing touches that precede its departure.

Above: The launch of the *uru* is an arduous process and extends into the night when the tide is high. It is time for the *uru* to prove its credentials and sail perfectly balanced into the sea after months of painstaking labour.

Left: In Beypore, a goat is sacrificed before the launch of the *Al Khalafi*, an *uru* bound for the Middle East. The meat will go into *biryani*, a dish made with rice and spices cooked along with the meat, and will be served to the community.

amount of interest in Beypore around the project, to most of its population the ship Ki-en-gi (Sumerian for Land of the Master of Reeds) was just another one of the ships constructed.

What to them seems commonplace is in truth a phenomenon. Millions of rupees exchange hands as a matter of daily activity here, for Beypore is one among the last few places in the world where boats are still being fashioned out of wood. There are orders from all parts of the world for all types of vessels: cargo ships, ketches, yachts, barges and even a ship that was meant to be a floating restaurant. The most common vessel that comes out of Beypore is a cargo ship modelled according to grain clipper ships of 18th-century Europe. The modern version, however, runs on engine power in spite of its sails.

Though the master artisans use certain Sanskrit *shlokas*, or prayers and invocations, to guide them, none of it

is on paper. The art of boatbuilding remains a closely guarded secret handed down from father to son. Only a handful of such master craftsmen are left. Four to be precise.

Just as Kerala has its seafaring people, it has its backwater people too. A great part of Kerala lives along these backwaters, which stretch over 1,900 km long. They snake over the land, bequeathing paddy fields with good harvests and linking remote, isolated villages with crowded town pockets.[14]

The backwaters become the cynosure of the eyes of the world from August to September every year, when

Above: The backwaters are large inland lakes that ribbon across Kerala. They cover an area of over 1,900 km via a network of lagoons, lakes and 44 rivers and are a lifeline of irrigation and drinking water.

Right: Sunlight streams into a narrow stretch of the backwaters as part of the daily tide of the rising and setting sun.

the celebrated Snake Boat Races, a water regatta unique to Kerala, takes place. Every year thousands of people crowd the water's edge to cheer the huge black crafts as they slice through the waters to a spectacular finish. Not all of them know what the origin of the tradition is. Or why it came to be. Nevertheless in their exuberance for the sport, the sanctity of a tradition is preserved. Perhaps that is what makes Kerala unique. Its traditions and the irrepressible need in a Malayali to follow some of these traditions, if not all of them.

Above and far left: The cacophony of sellers marketing their catch and buyers haggling resounds through and beyond the immediate environs of this fish market in Alappuzha.

Left: "How about a fight, a sword fight?", jests the fisherman as he thrusts his fish back and forth in response to the photographer, who is moving forward and backward to get the right composition. Mornings are an especially busy time at fish markets across Kerala as the newly-arrived catch is up for sale.

Above and right: Duck farming in Kottayam. Duck farming is a common sight in Kerala's backwaters. The ducks are usually fenced in but are let out to feed and also serve as playmates to children larking about in the waters. Dried shrimps are scattered into the waters as bait for fish that are quickly devoured by the ducks. The ducks are reared both for their eggs, which are larger than chickens' eggs, and their meat.

Preceding page, left: At Fort Kochi in Ernakulam, crows compete with fishermen for the catch and are often triumphant. The catch is heaved into baskets and sold in no time at markets adjacent to the fishing area.

Preceding page, right: Chinese fishing nets were introduced to Kerala between 1350 and 1450 by traders from the court of Kublai Khan, who became the first emperor of China's Mongol dynasty in 1260 and was the grandson of warrior-ruler Genghis Khan. More than 600 years after they were first used in Kerala, the nets are still a source of livelihood to hundreds of fishermen here.

Above and right: Families living along the backwater families is boats, and it is a matter backwaters are dependent on itinerant vendors, of great pride for a family to own one. Simple whose boats are often piled temptingly with ambitions and simple lives characterise the wares, for their day-to-day needs. backwater residents.

Preceding page: A boat sits idle next to a house *Next page, left:* A houseboat lingers on the in the backwaters of Kumarakom in Kottayam. stillness of Vembanad Lake. Docked near The number of coconut trees growing on the the Taj Garden Retreat in Kumarakom, the house premises often measures the wealth houseboat is known locally as *kettuvallam* and of a Keralan family. The mode of transport for is an attractive accommodation option.

Next page, right: In Alappuzha, two boats are ingeniously combined using a wooden plank to transport a car across the backwaters. In a land crisscrossed by rivers, ferries are mandatory in many parts of Kerala where road access is unavailable, and they are often used to transport heavier vehicles such as trucks and buses.

ആചാരങ്ങൾ

TRADITIONS

Left: A Kathakali performer replete with
costume, make-up and headaddress.

Given the various foreign influences
that pervade Kerala, it would be
natural to assume that the Malayali is
a cultural mongrel. Instead one
discovers a people who, despite the
comings and goings of the world into
their shores, are sticklers for tradition.
Family reunions, festivals and
weddings all have their own mores just
as the everyday has its. A visit to the
tea shop in villages is as customary as
the daily newspaper. A ramble through
the streets is as habitual as a quick
discussion on world politics and local
affairs. As for food, most Malayalis
think of themselves as gourmands and
will insist that there is nothing as
delicious as Malayali food cooked the
traditional way.

Ayurveda, which means the science
of life, took shape in India in the second
millennium B.C. It is a holistic approach
to a person's health and offers not only
remedies to ailments, but also to their
prevention. For thousands of years
Kerala has preserved this ancient
tradition in its most authentic form
through a long lineage of traditional
practitioners and vast natural resources
of medicinal herbs.[15]

Yet another tradition originates
from Ayurveda: the ancient martial art
of Kalaripayattu. *Kalari* means venue
of training and *payattu*, martial arts.
Though its exact origin is obscure,

Kalaripayattu is acknowledged as one of the oldest martial arts in the world. There is a legend about a Buddhist monk who studied Kalaripayattu in India during one of his travels and passed on his skills upon returning to Shaolin in China. Hence Kalaripayattu is said to be the originator of all other forms of martial arts. Kalaripayattu equips its practitioners not only with the skill to fight, but also the skill to heal, linking the art with Ayurveda.[16]

Kerala's two most famous dance forms are Kathakali and Mohiniattam. Kathakali, literally meaning story-play, is a dance drama that Kerala conceived in the 17th century. Kathakali combines five forms of fine art: literature, music, painting, acting and dance.[17] As much as Kathakali is an art performed exclusively by men, Mohiniattam is an art reserved for women. Mohiniattam is a classical solo dance of sheer enchantment with a very sensual undertone. In Hindu mythology Lord Vishnu took the form of Mohini, the divine enchantress, to divert the attention of havoc-wreaking demons. The dance derives its name from this divine character.[18]

Just as its dance forms, painting too had its genius and impact that percolated into the everyday life of the Malayali. Raja Ravi Varma, Kerala's most renowned painter who lived between 1848 and 1906, illustrated enchantresses, maidens, kings, scholars, gods and goddesses. In fact in a lot of Hindu homes in Kerala it is the renditions of Ravi Varma's gods and goddesses that are worshipped.

And it is this then that we must ask: in a land so steeped in tradition and so exposed to change, who are the gods and goddesses?

Left: A group of labourers in Alappuzha indulge in an extended break. Two activities are emblematic of Keralan streetlife: men engrossed in the day's newspapers and groups of men casually observing the advance of life around them.

Far left: Posing proudly in front of his teashop, this typical Keralan is content to tend his shop and observe the intricacies of day-to-day life across his shop counter.

Next page: The Panchavadyam musical performance is unique to Kerala. It involves five percussion instruments and a conch. Pictured here are Edappan Appunni and Group.

Above: Leela Cletus, a beaming Christian bride in Alappuzha is flanked by her equally exultant parents just moments before her wedding ceremony. Santosh Mani, her husband-to-be, works and lives in the Middle East. The incidence of arranged marriages like this one, once the norm in Kerala as in India, is gradually on the decline.

Right: The photographer enjoys a lighthearted moment with silk-swathed relatives at his ancestral house in Kozhikode and revisits memories of many late nights spent in this room as an eager, young photography student. The Kanchipuram silk saris of southern India are a measure of wealth and status in Kerala. From left to right: The photographer, Sudhir Ramchandran; his mother, Vimala Ramachandran; aunt, Rema Valsan; uncle, Valsan; cousin, Bina Valsan; and aunt, Seetha.

Above: Traditionally cooked in cylindrical bamboo shoot steamers, *puttu*, made from coarse rice powder and coconut, is a typical breakfast food and usually eaten with a spicy *kadala*, or chickpea, curry. For the sweet-toothed, the chickpea curry is replaced with bananas and generous sprinklings of sugar.

Right: Idiappam, or string hoppers, are steamed bunches of fluffy rice noodles that are eaten smothered in a rich potato or meat stew.

Preceding page: Kerala *paratha* are layered pancakes made from kneaded and rolled flour that is thinned by tossing it in the air. Several layers are then combined and browned on a sizzling griddle. They are most often dipped into a keenly-spiced meat curry.

Left: Not for the faint-tongued, these prawns are dusted liberally with chili powder and sautéed to a delicious crisp.

Above: The *sadya* is a smorgasbord of vegetarian delights. It is a traditional Keralan meal served on banana leaves at weddings and festival celebrations and can consist of up to 23 dishes. The positioning of the banana leaf and the order of serving the *sadya* dishes are precise. The *sadya*, like most Indian food, is eaten with one's right hand.

Ayurveda is a revered Indian healing tradition that dates back to the second millennium B.C. The words *ayur* and *veda* mean life and knowledge of respectively, and Ayurveda is essentially a treatise on the science of healthy living. Ayurveda was scoffed at by the British during their occupation of India but has now gained considerable popularity both domestically and internationally. The tradition has spawned the burgeoning industry of Ayurveda tourism.

Above left: An Ayurvedic massage in progress at Spice Village, a resort in Thekkady.

Above centre: Treatments are gleaned from palm-leaf inscriptions that are a few thousand years old.

Above right: Gigantic vats are used to prepare Ayurvedic medicines at scorching temperatures in a pharmacy.

Left: A selection of Ayurvedic herbs.

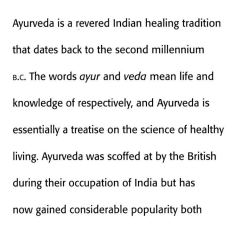

Ayurvedic treatment is much more effective during the monsoon season, when the body is cool and more responsive. Treatments are broadly divided into the rejuvenation, prevention and restoration categories. These treatments use natural herbs with each person meriting a different treatment based on his or her *prakruthi*, or unique genetic code.

Above: Ancient porcelain urns are used to mature the concoctions for Ayurvedic treatments at a traditional pharmacy.

Left: Staff pack Ayurvedic medicine at a traditional pharmacy near Kozhikode city.

Left: Between 10 and 12 hours go into the application of the intricate make-up and donning of the elaborate costumes for a Kathakali performance. The make-up is all-natural and is created from powdered minerals, spices, coconut oil and the saps and barks of certain trees and fruits. Eggplant flower seeds are inserted under the performers' eyelids to make their eyes appear bloodshot and provide a vivid contrast to the green make-up.

Far left: Kathakali artists perform at the Brunton Boatyard in Fort Kochi. Kathakali is a bewitching synergy of five forms of art: *sahithyam* (literature), *sangeetham* (music), *chithram* (painting), *natyam* (acting) and *nritham* (dance). Kathakali is usually performed in temple precincts and a single performance can extend over 10 days—one act is played out every night from dusk till daybreak.

Left: Kathakali artists apply their own make-up before a performance.

Kathakali themes are drawn from the wealth of Indian mythology and delineate the intrigues of interactions between the three worlds of gods, humans and demons. The entire story is told through the language of hand gestures and body and eye movements to the accompaniment of a vocal and instrumental score. There are five types of costumes and make-up that define the characters in any Kathakali performance. They are *pacha* (green), *kathi* (knife), *thadi* (beard), *kari* (black) and *minukku* (polished). The *chokanna thadi* (black beard) make-up, for example, represents aggressive and demonical characters. Kathakali is performed only by men.

Left and above: Mohiniattam is a classical solo dance form, performed above by Aruna Marar, that combines the grace of Bharathanatyam (a dance form native to the neighbouring state of Tamil Nadu) and the dynamism of Kathakali. Performed only by women, it originated as a temple dance performed by Devadasis—young girls whose parents betrothed them to temple

deities. The dance depicts the different incarnations of feminine love and carries an air of eroticism. Temple festivals are the usual occasions for a Mohiniattam performance.

Preceding page: A whirling dance tableau by the Daksha Sheth Dance Company. The company is considered one of the most daring

and contemporary troupes in India. In a land where artists rarely veer away from traditional dance forms, Daksha Sheth, a renowned exponent of the northern Indian classical dance form, Kathak, has experimented with Kalaripayattu and Chhau, a dance of eastern India. Like Kathakali, Chhau dancers remain silent and are accompanied by instruments.

All pictures: Kalaripayattu exponents in Nettoor spurn gravity in airborne face-offs. Kalaripayattu is considered as one the oldest martial arts in the world. Legend has it that Kalaripayattu was developed by Parasurama, the founder of Kerala, who taught the art to 21 disciples for the protection of the newborn territory. Kalaripayattu has a deep spiritual core with an emphasis on protection as opposed to aggression. Influences of Kalaripayattu have been borrowed and integrated into traditional dance forms such as Kathakali.

Next page: Narayanan Embranthiri dazzles the eye with his stupefying demonstration of the Kalaripayattu technique of keeping predators away from cattle. Narayanan has taken over from his father as the *gurukkal* or head teacher at the ENS Kalari Centre in Ernakulam.

Left: Brilliantly caparisoned elephants are anchored in an adoring sea of humanity at the Thrissur Pooram Festival, the largest annual Festival in India with almost a million attendees. The festival, which takes place in April, is a lighthearted duel between two temples, the Thiruvambady Krishna Temple and the Paramekavu Devi Temple, to determine which one can parade the best-looking elephants. Each temple fields 15 elephants decorated with glittering frontlets, regal parasols, peacock plume fans and yak-tail whisks. There are families in Thrissur that for generations have dedicated themselves to producing the various adornments for this particular festival. The highlight of the festival is the Kudamattam, during which the parasols are raised in turn over the elephants on either side to the thunderous roaring of the crowds. A dazzling display of fireworks and street shows forms part of the weeklong buildup to the Thrissur Pooram Festival.

Above: Tempers and temperatures cohere into the annual exhilaration that is the Aranmula Boat Race. The spectacle consists of around 26 *palliyodam,* or snake boats, thrusting down the Pamba River. Each boat is over 30 feet in length and accommodates four helmsmen, 100 rowers and 25 singers whose exhortational rhythm is echoed by the thousands of spectators. More a celebration than a competition, the Aranmula Boat Race marks the Onam festival.

Above: Raja Ravi Varma was a Keralan artist best known for his renditions of Hindu religious icons and scenes from Indian epics. His paintings of Indian women idealised the female form and were, for many years, the definitive Indian standard for feminine beauty.

Left: A Raja Ravi Varma mural of scenes from the *Mahabharata* animates a wall at the Kudira Malika Palace in Thiruvananthapuram.

GODS

Left: Krishna Jayanthi celebrations take place in Kozhikode. A 4-km-long procession of boys dressed as Lord Krishna, called a *Shoba Yatra*, winds its way to a Lord Krishna temple. Part of the celebrations depict scenes from the life of Krishna, including his mischievous exploits of breaking mud pots to treat himself to handfuls of his favourite snack of warm butter.

In Kerala, god assumes many forms. Over the years, all faiths of the world have come to Kerala and in its richness found a resting place and a haven, making it possible for all these faiths to be amalgamated with the existing forms of worship without losing their religious character. Perhaps that is the reason why in Kerala so many religions coexist in peace.

One of the foreign religions that arrived in Kerala was Judaism. The Kochi Jews claim that 10,000 Jews fled to Kerala after the Second Temple of Jerusalem was destroyed in A.D. 70. The Jewish community was ravaged by the Portuguese but left alone by the Dutch and British.

When the State of Israel was established in 1948, most of the Jews in Kochi left. Only a few hundred remained. Today the number of Jews has dwindled even further and most of them are elderly people.[19]

Christianity, in contrast, found a true home in Kerala. The Christians of Kerala today are divided into several branches: the Latin Catholic Church,

the Syro-Malabar Catholic Church, the Jacobite Syrian Church, the Nestorian Church, the Anglican Church, which is now part of the Church of South India, the Marthoma Syrian Church and the Syro-Malankara Catholic Church. In addition, there are also a number of minor churches and missions. The Syrian Christians of Kerala firmly believe that St. Thomas the Apostle is the father of Christianity in India. It is said that he landed at Maliankara near Kodungalloor in A.D. 52. He preached Christianity first to the Jews and then converted 12 Brahmin families.[20]

But it is Islam that had the strongest impact in Kerala. There was much trade between India and Arabia even before Prophet Muhammad's time. Ibn Dinar came to spread the word of Islam in Kerala and set up mosques across the state. From the 15th to the 17th centuries the Muslim population flourished. This undermined the traditional Hindu caste system, negated the social superiority of the Brahmins and the Nairs and helped increase the self-esteem of the lower classes.[21]

Jainism took root in Kerala through Emperor Chandragupta Maurya, who reigned from 321 to 297 B.C. Buddhism was born in India in the sixth century B.C. and propagated by Emperor Asoka's missionaries during his lifetime between 273 and 232 B.C.[22] The religion faded after Vedic Brahmins, who arrived in Kerala between A.D. 700 and A.D. 800, proved the intellectual superiority of Hinduism over Buddhism.[23]

Today there are more than 10,000 temples in Kerala, and each has its own festivities called *pooram*. Though many of these festivals are religious, there are secular ones such as Onam, the harvest festival held in honour of the legendary King Bali.

King Bali was a noble and pious ruler. He ruled the asuras well and tried to curb their violent behaviour. Unlike his ancestors, King Bali sought supremacy over heaven and earth by non-violent means. He undertook rigorous penance instead of going to battle with the gods. By the strength of his dedication and virtue, he wrested heaven away from Indra, the king of gods. Soon Bali was king of the earth, heaven and netherworld, and everyone on earth loved him dearly. There never had been such a noble king as Bali, it was said.

The gods soon grew jealous of King Bali and feared that they would lose their standing if he continued to reign. "The people don't turn to us in times of trouble because Bali takes such good care of them. Soon they will forget

Left: A small doorway belies the tunnelled potential of this dust-laden antique shop in Jew Town, Fort Kochi. Traditional masks, lamps, urns and engraved spice boxes are among some of the delights awaiting discovery.

Right: An avenue of antique shops populates the street leading to the Paradesi Synagogue. These shops are mandatory stops for both international and domestic tourists, who scour their premises for tempting bargains.

that we exist. As long as he continues to accrue such blessings, he'll be lord of the three worlds forever," the gods complained to Lord Vishnu, who was the protector and preserver of the world and restorer of moral order.

As if to convince Lord Vishnu, they added, "Bali is a good king but his children might not be such noble rulers. What then? They will destroy this universe if they inherit such enormous power!"

So Vishnu decided to step in and save the gods from further humiliation. He entered the world as Vamana, a child born to Sage Kasyapa and Aditi. Even as an adult, Vamana remained diminutive, and it was as a little man that he went to King Bali's court asking for alms. King Bali received Vamana as though he were a very important guest and asked, "What can I do for you? How can I be of service to you?"

Vamana looked up at the king and simply said, "All I need is three feet of land!"

"Is that all?" the king asked Vamana in surprise. "Don't you need anything more?"

"Three feet of land will do," Vamana said.

"Then it shall be yours. Do take it from wherever you want," the king said, feeling curious and amused by the little man's request.

Then as the king watched, the little man began to grow and soon he was as tall as the sky. With his left foot, he covered the earth. "This is the first

foot of land," Vamana said.

With his right foot, he covered the heavens. "This is the second foot. What is left, O King? Where shall I take my third foot of land from?"

King Bali realised that this was none other than Lord Vishnu and that the third foot of land had to be found. So he fell on his knees and bent his head, "All I have left is my head. Take this as the third foot of land," he said with quiet dignity.

When the gods saw this, even they were moved to tears and rained flowers on Bali. But Vamana put his foot on the king's head and pressed him down into the netherworld. "Henceforth, this shall be your kingdom," he told King Bali.

But just as King Bali was about to leave the earth for good, he saw the tears in his people's eyes and felt his own fill. "How can I stay away from my subjects?" he thought.

Then he turned to Vamana and said, "All I ask is that for one day in a year I be allowed to visit my people and know all is well with them."

Vamana agreed and, to this day, the people of Kerala welcome King Bali with

Left: The traditional Keralan architecture of the Munchunthi Palli Mosque in Kozhikode is indicative of the seamless assimilation of Islam into the ethos of Kerala.

Above: The Cheraman Juma Masjid in Kodungalloor was built by Hindu carpenters and masons in A.D. 629 upon the decree of the king of Kodungalloor. The very first mosques in Kerala were devoid of minarets and their gables were exquisitely carved in the fashion of Hindu temples. However, very few of these original structures remain as most were rebuilt to look like mosques in the Middle East.

Right: K.M. Haji Saidu Mohammed is a *mukri*, or muezzin, at the Cheraman Juma Masjid. He has dedicated his life to the mosque, having served there from a very young age.

a flower carpet and wait for his coming year after year. Every doorstep is adorned with beautiful and intricately-patterned floral decorations. Men, women and children wear new clothes, and within the homes there is the hustle and bustle of a traditional *sadya* being prepared.[1]

As someone said, "Life in Kerala is good. What is difficult is making a living there!"

Left: Muslim womenfolk pose with unusual candour outside an ancestral house in Malappuram. The Mappilas, or Malabar Muslims of Kerala, constitute 20 percent of the state's population and are one of the oldest Islamic communities in South Asia. They owe their origins to Arab traders and sailors. Unlike in North India, Islam was integrated peacefully into the fabric of Kerala as it arrived through trade and not conquest. Ibn Dinar was the man credited for first bringing Islam to Kerala.

Above: A priestess presides at the Mannarasala Sree Nagaraja Temple in Alappuzha. Amma, or Great Mother, the priestess, blesses devotees by cupping her hands in the shape of a cobra's hood. This ancient shrine is set in a serene jungle and is a renowned pilgrim centre dedicated to Nagaraja, the serpent god. A woman priestess with the exalted powers of Amma is a rarity in Kerala. She is known to cure infertility in women and leprosy, among other diseases. Any person bitten by a snake is rushed to the Amma's side for treatment inspired by her as-yet-unblemished success rate. Generations of Ammas have passed on the divine mantle to their successors since the first Amma was born in 1079.

Above: Snake worshippers lose themselves to the serpent god Nagaraja at a Hindu temple.

Right: Amma rests quietly after a frenzied ritual wherein she was supposedly possessed by the serpent deity of this temple in Kozhikode. When in this state she slithered about the temple grounds as a serpent would and leapt up frequently to spout prophecies to her ardent devotees, who stood by with bated breath.

At the Ganapathy Temple in Palakkad, freshly-
bathed priests and devotees proceed before
the crack of dawn into the misty inner rooms
where the idols reside to perform *pujas*,
or Hindu prayers. The Ganapathy Temple
is dedicated to Lord Ganesha, considered
to be the remover of all obstacles.

All pictures and next page, left: Millions of devotees from all over India perform arduous pilgrimage rites to pay homage to Lord Ayappa at the Ayappa Temple in Sabarimala, Pathanamthitta, every year. Lord Ayappa is said to be born as the result of a union between Lord Vishnu and Lord Shiva. A 40-mile trek completes six weeks of austere living modelled on the life of an ascetic. Pilgrims observe a regimen of strict vegetarianism, celibacy and abstinence from alcohol. They are required to sleep on the floor and shun the use of footwear. Lord Ayappa was a bachelor and the confines of his temple are forbidden to all women except those yet to attain puberty and those past menopause.

Above left: An Annaprasam ceremony at Guruvayoor Temple in Thrissur. The ceremony introduces babies to their first morsels of solid food. During this highly auspicious ceremony a Brahmin priest gives the children sips of holy water and smears their little foreheads with sandal paste. The parents then feed the children with mouthfuls of rice and *payasam*, a dessert often made with rice or lentils. It is believed that performing this ceremony will ensure that the children will never want for food in later life. The Guruvayoor Temple is Kerala's most important Hindu temple.

Above right: A priest balances a baby's weight in endowments to the Guruvayoor Temple as part of Thulabharam, a special ceremony conducted by Hindus that involves a donation of fruit, sugar, coconuts or sandalwood in accordance with one's weight to the deity of the temple. In ancient India maharajahs often weighed themselves against gold or silver coins to win the deity's favour. It is also possible for non-Hindus to perform Thulabharams.

Left: Hordes of schoolboys delight in the excitement of playing Lord Krishna for a day during Krishna Jayanthi celebrations. The festival is extremely popular in India and celebrates Krishna's birthday in August. Krishna is one of the most beloved Hindu gods.

Above: The chief Theyyam performer commands the hypnotic gaze of onlookers at the Sri Muthappan Temple in Kannur. There are hundreds of different types of Theyyam, a ritualistic folk dance exclusive to northern Kerala that has a tradition going back a thousand years. The headgear of the Theyyam performer can ascend to between 9 and 12 metres and the make-up has a base colour of striking orange with the eyes banded in black and the lips a savage red. The chief performer goes into a prophetic trance and answers questions put to him from the gathered crowd about their past, present and future. This temple is the only one in Kerala that conducts daily rituals of Theyyam performances. Unique to the Sri Muthappan Temple is the non-vegetarian and alcoholic offering, which is usually dried fish and a local liquor called toddy, made to the deity.

LIVING

Left: Workers roll beedies at the Sadhoo Beedi factory in Kannur. A beedi is an indigenous, filterless cigarette produced by rolling tobacco in a tendu leaf obtained from a tree that grows wild in central India. Around 55 percent of the tobacco smoked in India is consumed via beedis as they are considerably cheaper than cigarettes, which are more prevalent in cities. A growing export market for beedis has engendered a spectrum of foreign flavours that range from black liquorice and mandarin orange to lemon-lime and wild cherry.

Life in Kerala, as in everything else about it, is composed of a texture unlike anywhere else in India. And the greatest testimony to this is the houses in the state. From spartan concrete boxes to garishly ornate mansions, from ecofriendly Laurie Baker homes to the traditional tile, wood and laterite *tharavad*, the Malayali's abode shows a discrepancy in the composition of the society. And yet each Malayali is made of the same matter within.

This eclectic range of houses is matched by an equally confounding mix of statistics: Kerala has a 90 percent literacy rate, the highest per capita consumption of newspapers in India, a fertility rate of just 1.7 births per woman and a life expectancy of 72 years, which is much higher than the life expectancy of 61 years in the rest of India. Yet Kerala also has a per capita income that is lower than Cambodia's or Sudan's and an unemployment rate

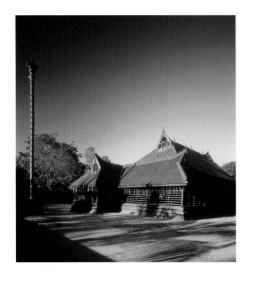

Left: Classical Keralan architecture and serene surroundings characterise Kerala Kalamandalam, which is an august academy of the arts responsible for the preservation of traditional folk art in Kerala. Students may be trained over a period of up to six years and can join performing groups that go on regular national and international cultural tours. The academy was founded in 1930 and is located in Cheruthuruthy, a small village in Thrissur.

Right: A *pathinarukettu* is a traditional house with 16 blocks built around a courtyard. Smaller variations are the *nallukettu*, or four-blocked house, and the *ettukettu*, or eight-blocked house. In the days when the caste system and untouchability were rife in Kerala, the upper castes communicated with the lower castes through the bars encircling the room.

that is one of the highest in India.[24]

In short, though Kerala is very poor, it manages to maintain a decent standard of living. This can be largely attributed to Communist policies implemented in 1957 when Communists won the elections in Kerala. The state was the first in the world to form a democratically elected communist government.[24]

For years, Kerala has survived on meagre income from the agricultural sector and cottage industries, which range from its legendary handlooms to terracotta tiles, from making beedis to banana chips and from the manufacture of rubber to coconut-based products. In fact, among the many tags Kerala has earned for itself, the most pertinent one is the money order economy. Most of the money reaching Kerala is sent from outside the state and specifically from its workers in the Middle East.[24]

Unlike the rest of India, Kerala has resisted industrialisation. This may prove untenable in the long run, and the state might have to accept some degree of industrialisation eventually. The challenge is to do so without eroding the natural splendour or quality of everyday life, which in many ways is still idyllic. All one needs to do is to take a walk through a village in Kerala to understand just why the state defies description or pigeonholing of any kind.

Let's begin with the outskirts. At a house by the fields and in the

distance are shadowy peaks. The earth is black and moist, and all day a cool breeze blows and lifts worries and anxieties away. The lushness of the vegetation, both wild and cultivated, adds to the tranquillity of the place.

Midway is the village *kavu*, or sacred grove. In the winter months, just as the moon shines with a particular brilliance, so does the Velluchapad's, or oracle's, fortunes. An offering is made every night, and the Velluchapad is a busy man. Meanwhile the RSS Pracharaks go about their drill in the temple grounds.

At the other end of the village is the *vayanashala*, or reading room. There are rows of books—some tattered and old, while others are still fragrant with printer's ink. Adolf Hitler's *Mein Kampf* sits cheek by jowl with Mahatma Gandhi's *The Story of My Experiments with Truth*. There are at least a thousand books in this little reading room, and all it costs a person to use the library is 29 rupees a year.

And then appears the first contradiction. The noise. Pure rant is the resonance of Kerala. Its chief instrument is the trumpet-shaped loudspeaker, or *kolambi*, as the villagers refer to it.

Long before even the birds wake up, the *kolambi* spews out devotional songs from the village *kavu*. Then there is a long silence that is broken by a riot of birdcalls. This is soon followed by sounds that signal the commencement of the day's activities. Jeeps begin to prowl hither and thither to advertise new shops, political meetings, a film release, lottery tickets, eye camps and so on. Everyday there is something to blare about!

Then arrive the vendors. The fish vendor has a cry that is a hoot turned into a call, and he is ably supported by an air horn. As the day wears out, the sounds of faith take their turn at commanding the airwaves. The *kolambi* hisses and splutters. In most villages, this has become the equivalent of a factory siren. Workers put down their hoes, ploughs, knives and spades and begin to walk home as the songs drown all noise, natural and otherwise. A short while later sermons begin in a mosque at the other end of the village and continue into the night.

Then rant dwindles to quiet. The cicadas begin their shrill song, and in the sky Sirius glows brighter than ever. These are the only invariables in a state where the only thing constant about life is change.[1]

The Kudira Malika Palace, or Horse Palace, was named for the line of prancing horses that support the roof of the top floor. The palace has been restored and converted into a museum displaying traditional artefacts and a collection of royal family paintings.

Left: Siblings Sujeesh and Radhika are quizzed by their mother, M.K. Sumathi, on what they have learnt in school that day as part of a daily routine. This maternal concern is a vital part of Kerala's tradition of education.

Right: Schoolchildren in Alappuzha on a break from class. Tourists, greeted with persistent cries of "Pen, miss!" from hordes of schoolchildren in Kerala as opposed to demands for money or food in other parts of the country, will vouch for the triumph of the state's education system.

Below right: Reading the daily newspaper is almost a religious activity in Kerala among the young and old. Kerala is the most literate state in India with an overall literacy level of 90 percent. Unique to the state are government-owned and privately-run reading rooms, where people retire to read and discuss matters of interest— politics being a favourite topic.

tourism industry have been quick to capitalise on its new-found international appeal.

Right: The owner of a roadside tea stall in Kottayam performs his rendition of the famed four-foot tea with typical nonchalance. The four-foot tea involves the dual tasks of mixing the tea, sugar and milk as well as cooling it to prevent scalded tongues. Exponents of the four-foot tea can be found across Kerala. Tea is one of the most popular beverages in the state.

Above: The myriad foreign occupations of Kerala are evident along a walk down Fort Kochi's streets in Ernakulam. Buildings reflect in turn the influences of the Dutch, Portuguese, British and Chinese presence in Kochi and imbue the street with a multicultural appeal.

Top: Windy palms preside over a yoga session at the Marari Beach Resort in the village of Mararikulam. Yoga is an ancient Indian practice aimed at uniting the body, mind and soul. In recent years yoga has attracted a considerable following in the West, and players in Kerala's

Preceding page: Children out on a school picnic on Kappad beach climb to an elevated point to view the Arabian Sea.

Left: The photographer's favourite aunt, Seetha Teacher as she was known to all, was wedded to her profession. She taught for almost 50 years. Many of her students are now successfully employed in different parts of the world. The photographer remembers many happy days spent studying photography by the window of this room with his aunt absorbed in religious reading in the foreground.

Above: Long-time Kannur resident Mrs. Balagopal cherishes rare moments with her holidaying daughter-in-law Sulekha and grandchildren Premalatha and Partha.

Dr. Sulekha Randhir, a first-generation immigrant to Kuwait, is one of the millions of Indians in the Persian Gulf. Kerala alone has exported about two million members of her workforce to the Middle East. Signs of Gulf money are evident in the sprawling houses and affluent lifestyle of Gulf returnees.

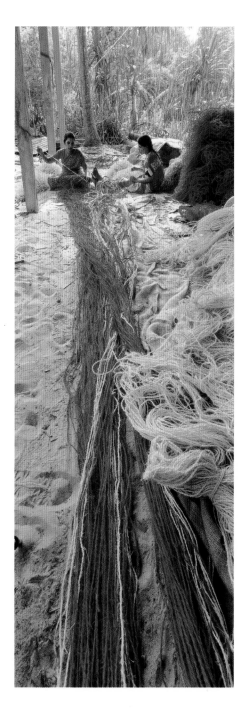

Above: Handloom fabrics are shipped to all over the world from the modest interiors of Commonwealth Trust (India) Ltd, or ComTrust, in Kozhikode. The pioneering ComTrust fabrics are internationally prized for their quality and variety. The word calico is derived from the old name for the city of Kozhikode, which was Calicut.

Left: The coir industry provides employment to half a million people in Kerala. Coir is a fibre produced from the husk of the coconut. The husk is separated from the coconut, soaked in water for a period of up to 10 months, beaten with a mallet and spun on a loom to produce a variety of household and personal utilities, from doormats and carpets to wall hangings and footwear. India is the third-largest coconut-producing country in the world.

Far left: Bell metal is fired in Alappuzha to produce artefacts ranging from the religious to the quotidian—from temple or church bells and lamps to cooking utensils and serving plates. Brass, tin and copper form an alloy from which the different products are fashioned. Bell metal crafting is another of Kerala's family-centred professions, passed on practically and orally from generation to generation. The younger generation's pursuit of more lucrative professions poses a grave threat to the survival of the art.

Above: PNC Menon with his wife. Founder of a conglomerate synonymous with state-of-the-art construction, PNC Menon is a Malayali who has come back to pay tribute to his roots. His Middle Eastern corporation, the Services and Trade Company, incarnated in India as Sobha Developers and has revolutionised the construction industry with its world-class standards.

Left: The much-feted Captain C.P. Krishnan Nair, chairman of Leela Palaces and Resorts, is a pioneer nonpareil in both the garment and hospitality industries.

Preceding page, left: Painter and sculptor Yusuf Arakkal meditates on a roller-coaster life that saw him go from pounding the pavements of Bangalore to being one of the most revered Indian artists of the 20th century. He has held solo exhibitions all over the world and credits his success to hard work and self-belief.

Preceding page, right: Balan Nambiar's art is fed by the deep roots of his tradition, particularly the ritual art form of Theyyam. Balan's creative energy finds expression in sculpture, painting and photography. His art resides in museums and private collections across the globe.

Body Text Bibliography

1 *Magical Indian Myths*. Anita Nair, Puffin Books, India.

2 www. shelterbelt.com/KJ/khprasuram.html

3 kerala-history.nrksite.com

4 traveltoindianet.com/history-of-kerala.html

5 members.tripod.com/anil_varghese/hland.html

6 www.kerala.com/kera/travel.htm

7 www.kerala.cc/keralahistory/index6.htm

8 www.kerala.indianvisit.com/wildlife/silent_valley

9 www.keralaonline.com/travelindex.asp?cap=thwild

10 kerala.indianvisit.com/beaches/index.html

11 www.theindiatravel.com/cityguide/state/kerala/beaches.html

12 www.kerala.indianvisit.com/destinations/quilon

13 www.bartleby.com/65/ca/calico.html

14 kerala.indianvisit.com/backwaters/index.html

15 www.healthlibrary.com/news/1-6jan2001/times-ayurveda1.htm

16 www.kalaripayattu.org/history.htm

17 www.sholay.com/culture

18 www.indianest.com/dances/00108.htm

19 www.kerala.cc/keralahistory/index35.htm

20 www.kerala.cc/keralahistory/index36.htm

21 www.kerala.cc/keralahistory/index37.htm

22 search.eb.com

23 www.kerala.cc/keralahistory/index34.htm

24 www.theatlantic.com/issues/98sep/kerala.htm

Caption Bibliography

WEBSITES

ayurveda.indianvisit.com

campus.northpark.edu

coconutboard.nic.in

elephant.elehost.com

in.biz.yahoo.com

krpcds.org

skepdic.com

teacher.scholastic.com

travel.indiamart.com

us.rediff.com

www.acorn-deepika.com

www.alappuzha.com

www.all-india-tour-travel.
    com

www.allkeralatours.com

www.american.edu

www.ayurveda-herbs.com

www.ayurvedic.org

www.ayyappan-ldc.com

www.balannambiar.com

www.bigshots.com.au

www.bismicoir.com

www.blonnet.com

www.capitalmarket.com

www.cardamomcityindia.
    com

www.casinogroup.com

www.censusindia.net

www.cmicongregation.org

www.cochin.org

www.dailyexcelsior.com

www.eindiatourism.com

www.evesindia.com

www.financialexpress.com

www.flonnet.com

www.freethechildren.org

www.hinduonnet.com

www.humnri.com

www.idukki.net

www.indiaagronet.com

www.indiainfoline.com

www.indianchristianity.com

www.indianembassy.org

www.indianmirror.com

www.indianspices.com

www.indiantravelinfo.com

www.indianvisit.com

www.indiaprofile.com

www.indiatravelinfo.com

www.indiatravelite.com

www.indiavarta.com

www.inika.com/arakkal

www.iyengar-yoga.com

www.kanjirappally.com

www.kannurtourism.org

www.kau.edu

www.kerala.com

www.kerala-hub.com

www.keralaeverything.com

www.klresort.com

www.kumarakom.com

www.midastreads.com

www.qjada.com

www.rediff.com

www.rubbermark.com

www.saranamayyappa.org

www.shelterbelt.com

www.smokeshopmag.com

www.sobhadevelopers.com

www.sundaykaumudi.com

www.tajhotels.com

www.thehorizons.com

www.thekkady.com

www.theleela.com

www.tribuneindia.com

www.trichurpooram.com

www.unep-wcmc.org

www.veesquare.com

www.webindia123.com

www1.cs.columbia.edu

Publications

Dance (Classic India Series). Ashish Khokar, Rupa & Co., 1994.

Dasha Avatar. India Book House Private Limited, 2001.

Discover Wayanad 'The Green Paradise'. District Tourism Promotion Council Wayanad, 1995.

Dravidian Kinship. Thomas R. Trautmann, Cambridge University Press, 1981.

Explore Kerala Travel Guide. Explore & Travel, 1998.

Facets of a Hundred Years Planting. Amita Baig and William Henderson, Tata Finley Limited, 1978.

Festivals of Kerala. P.J. Varghese, K.R. Ramachandran and P.S. Kurian, Tourist Desk, Cochin, 1993.

Important Birds of Periyar. Forestry Information Bureau, Kerala Forestry Department, 1995.

Kerala. The Guidebook Company Limited, 1993.

Kerala—Colours, Culture & Lifestyle. Salim Pushpanath and Ajay Marar, DEE BEE Info Publications, 2000.

Kerala Festivals. Salim Pushpanath and Ajay Marar, DEE BEE Info Publications, 1997.

Kerala—The Green Miracle. Salim Pushpanath & Ajay Marar, DEE BEE Info Publications.

Kerala: The Spice Coast of India. Raghubir Singh, Thames & Hudson, 1986.

Kerala—Tourists' Handbook. DEE BEE Info Publications, 1994.

Malabar Manual Volumes I & II. William Logan, Asian Educational Services, 1951.

Mattancherry Palace. Shivananda Venkatarao and Raman Namboodri, Archaeological Survey of India, Government of India, 1997.

Our Progress—A Bird's Eye View: 1902-1994. The Arya Vaidya Sala, Kottakkal.

Performing Arts of Kerala. Pankaj Shah & Mallika Sarabhai, Mapin Publishing Private Limited, 1994.

Seven Sacred Rivers. Bill Aitken, Penguin Books, 2003.

The Great Mother. Manasa Publications, 1991.

Theyyam Guide. District Tourism Promotion Council Kannur, 2000.

Tourism Directory of Kerala. Priyan C. Ooman, Global Communications, 1995.

Tourism Travel Directory of Kerala. United Communications, 1996.

These books provide valuable additional information on Kerala. However, most of them were produced in India and may not be available in other countries.

Index

agriculture 19, 20, 24, 25, 27, 29, 30, 33, 34, 37, 38, 42, 46, 47, 56, 59, 64, 74, 80, 93, 95, 131, 135, 136, 138, 144, 149
  cardamom 20, 30, 33, 37
  cashew 33
  coconut 27, 30, 33, 34, 38, 56, 59, 74, 95, 131, 136, 149
  coffee 30, 33, 38
  paddy 24, 25, 27, 30, 34, 64
  pepper 20, 29, 30, 33
  rubber 30, 33, 34, 136
  tea 19, 30, 33, 38, 42, 81, 144
  tapioca 30
  tobacco 135
Alappuzha 34, 67, 74, 81, 84, 123, 141, 149
Alleppey 53, 57
Arabian Sea 20, 27, 33, 53, 61, 144
Ayurveda 50, 79, 80, 91, 93

backwaters 27, 30, 33, 59, 64, 70, 74
Beypore 57, 59, 61, 63, 64

education 42, 53, 133, 119, 141, 147
Ernakulam 49, 59, 70, 113, 144

fish 30, 33, 49, 53, 56, 59, 67, 70, 133, 138
flora, 19, 20, 30, 38, 42, 44, 95, 138
food 46, 53, 56, 63, 70, 79, 88, 89, 129, 131, 136
Fort Kochi 37, 61, 70, 95, 113, 114, 144

Idukki 44

Kalaripayattu 30, 79, 80, 101, 102
Kathakali 30, 79, 80, 95, 96, 101, 102
Kappad 29, 57, 144
Kochi 29, 37, 49, 53, 59, 61, 144
Kodungalloor 113, 120
Kollam 53, 59
Kottayam 33, 59, 70, 74
Kovalam 50, 53, 56, 57
Kozhikode 30, 57, 59, 84, 93, 119, 120, 124, 149

Kudira Malika Palace 109, 138

literacy 30, 33, 119, 135, 138, 141

Malabar 29, 123
Malappuram 123
Malayalam 30
Malayali 30, 47, 66, 79, 80, 135, 152
Mohiniattam 80, 101
monsoon 49, 50, 53, 93
Munnar 38, 42
Muziris 29, 59

Palakkad 33, 46, 127
Parasurama 19, 20, 102
port 29, 57

Raja Ravi Varma 80, 109
religions 19, 20, 25, 30, 34, 64, 80, 84, 96, 101, 102, 107, 111, 113, 114, 119, 120, 123, 124, 127, 131, 133, 138, 147, 149
  Buddhism 80, 113
  Christianity 30, 34, 84, 113, 119

Hinduism 19, 20, 25, 30, 64, 80, 96, 101, 107, 111, 113, 114, 119, 120, 123, 124, 127, 129, 131, 133, 138, 149
Islam 113, 120, 123, 138
Jainism 113
Judaism 111, 113, 114

Silent Valley 42, 46

Thekkady 37, 44, 46, 91
Thiruvananthapuram 53, 109
Thrissur 131, 136

Vasco da Gama 29, 57

wildlife 20, 25, 27, 30, 34, 38, 40, 42, 44, 46, 47, 107
  deer 20, 38
  elephants 20, 25, 30, 34, 38, 42, 44, 46, 107
  gaur 38, 44
  Nilgiri tahr 38, 44, 46
  sambar 40
  squirrel 40
  tiger 38
Western Ghats 27, 33, 42

Sudhir Ramchandran

is an advertising and editorial photographer of

international standing.

Photo Credits
Above : Neha Diddee
Left   : M.K. Haridas
Pages 9 and 13 : On location photos by Sanjay Ramachandran,
Neha Diddee, M.K. Haridas, G. Kumaran and Tony Ooi Kok Pin.

Biography

Sudhir Ramchandran was born in Tanzania and migrated to India in his youth, and for the past three decades these multicultural roots have influenced his photography of the world.

A ceaseless innovator and tenacious perfectionist in the field of imaging, Sudhir has conceptualised and executed pioneering imaging projects all over the world. Since 1983 he has created hugely successful holistic workshops, the Compression Curve and NewSchool series, which saw expositions of some of the world's keenest creative minds in the fields of fashion, advertising, writing, design, photography and the digital arts. He is a popular lecturer on the photography circuit and holds regular workshops and seminars at various universities. He has nurtured interns from New York University, New York; Parsons School of Design, New York; and the National Institute of Design, Ahmedabad, among others.

He works with formats ranging from 8"x10"s to 35 mms and has been involved in numerous commercial and personal projects, many of which have won national and international awards including the FAO Gold Medal from the United Nations Educational, Scientific and Cultural Organisation (UNESCO). He was president of the Advertising and Industrial Photographers Association (AIPA) of India and Ambassador to the World Council of Professional Photographers (WCPP).

Sudhir's personal work consists primarily of beautiful international landscapes and people. His work has appeared in several leading international publications including *National Geographic Magazine*, premier books on India such as *Spectacular India* by Mapin Publishing Pvt. Ltd., and the prestigious Christie's London publication, *Costumes and Textiles of Royal India*. He is a frequent contributor to various magazines including Newsweek, *Architectural Digest, Interiors, Society, Asian Photography* and *India Today*.

Apart from commissioned projects that include the large format Mysore Palace publication and an upcoming book on the World Heritage Site of the Vijayanagar Empire, Sudhir has produced a series of pictorial essays on the Nilgiris that have been commissioned by Needle Industries India Pvt. Ltd. and reproduced as calendars. These calendars are a visual homage to the vanishing lifestyles and landscapes of the Nilgiris in South India. His love for spaces and people has ensured long-standing clients in the architectural and advertising fields including the Sheraton, the Taj and the Leela Group of Palaces and Resorts , and the Singapore Tourism Board.

Sudhir's work is a kinetic mix of images of surreal beauty and editorial immediacy. He is currently developing a body of work that arrests the swirl and spirit of India in eloquently composed panoramic format images.

Sudhir lives in Bangalore, India, with his wife and three children. He works out of offices in Singapore, Bangalore and London.

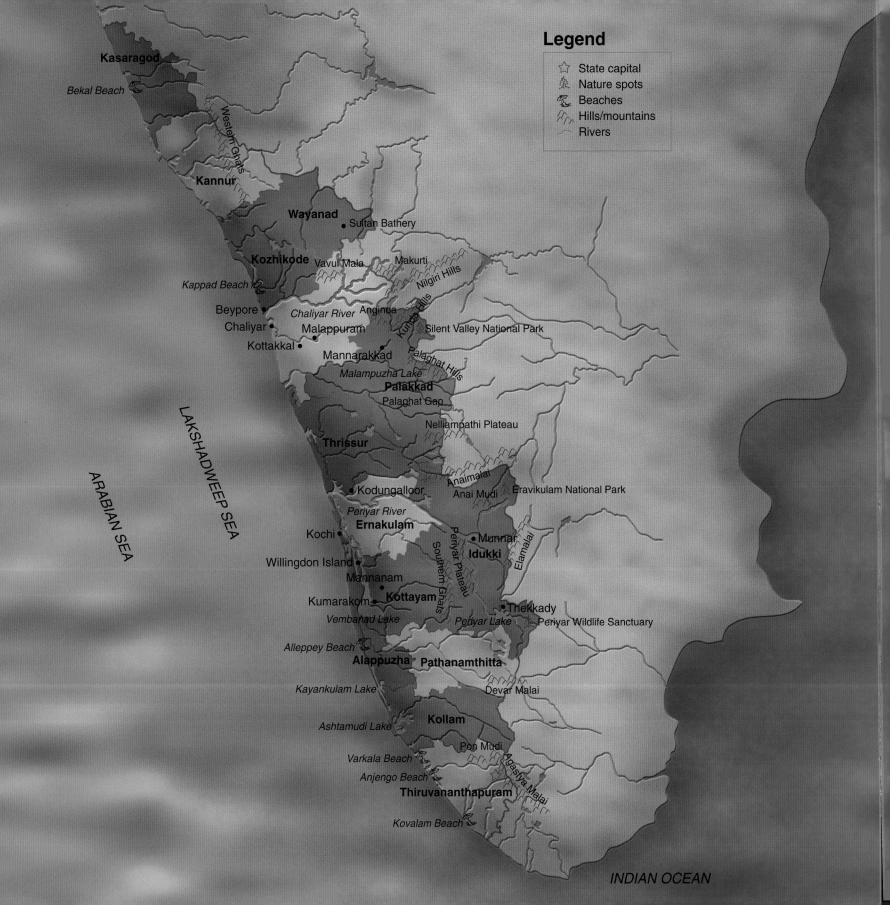